Night Light

A Book About the Moon

by Dana Meachen Rau   illustrated by Denise Shea

PICTURE WINDOW BOOKS
Minneapolis, Minnesota

Thanks to our advisers for their expertise, research, and advice:

Dr. Stanley P. Jones, Assistant Director
NASA-sponsored Classroom of the Future Program

Susan Kesselring, M.A., Literacy Educator
Rosemount–Apple Valley–Eagan (Minnesota) School District

Editorial Director: Carol Jones
Managing Editor: Catherine Neitge
Creative Director: Keith Griffin
Editor: Christianne Jones
Story Consultant: Terry Flaherty
Designer: Joe Anderson
Page Production: Picture Window Books
The illustrations in this book were created digitally.

Picture Window Books
5115 Excelsior Boulevard
Suite 232
Minneapolis, MN 55416
877-845-8392
www.picturewindowbooks.com

Printed in the United States of America.

Library of Congress Cataloging-in-Publication Data
Rau, Dana Meachen, 1971-
Night light : a book about the moon / by Dana Meachen Rau ; illustrated by
Denise Shea.
p. cm. — (Amazing science)
Includes bibliographical references and index.
ISBN 1-4048-1136-2 (hardcover)
ISBN 1-4048-1731-X (paperback)
1. Moon—Juvenile literature. I. Shea, Denise, ill. II. Title. III. Series.

QB582.R39 2006
523.3—dc22
                                                              2005003727

Table of Contents

Friends in Space

Do you have a best friend? Do you like to do lots of things together?

Earth and the moon are like best friends. The moon is Earth's closest neighbor in space. Earth and the moon are always together.

FUN FACT

The moon is traveling around Earth all the time.
It travels in an oval-shaped path called an orbit.

Gravity's Hold

Do you and your friend hold hands? Holding hands keeps you together.

Earth and the moon don't hold hands. They stay together with gravity. It is the force of Earth and the moon pulling on each other. This force keeps them from floating apart.

FUN FACT

Earth pulls on you, too! It keeps you from floating into the sky.

The Moon's Face

The moon has dark spots and light spots. Some people think the moon looks like a face. Have you ever looked for the man in the moon?

At night, the moon sometimes looks bright. The moonlight might be bright enough to make shadows on the ground. The moon does not produce light, though. Moonlight is really the sun's light bouncing off the moon.

FUN FACT

One side of the moon faces Earth. The other side faces away. From Earth, you can only see one side of the moon. You never get to see its other side.

Moon Phases

The moon sometimes looks like a bright circle. This circle is called a full moon.

The moon does not always look round. It looks like it gets smaller and thinner. Then it looks like it disappears! Keep watching. It will appear again soon. The moon starts small and thin. Then it grows until it is a circle again. These changes are called phases.

FUN FACT

The moon is not really changing shape. It just looks that way
from Earth. The sun shines on half of the moon at a time.
Phases are when we only see part of the moon's lit side.

Moon Rock

The moon is made of rock. There are many rocks floating in space. A long time ago, some of these rocks hit the moon.

The moon is covered with holes made by rocks crashing into it. These holes are called craters.

FUN FACT

The moon has flat and bumpy land areas. Tall
hills and mountains also rise from the ground.

Space Visits

People cannot live on the moon right now. There is no air to breathe.

People called astronauts have visited the moon. They wore special spacesuits. The suits had air inside so the astronauts could breathe.

FUN FACT

The astronauts weighed less on the moon than on Earth because of gravity. It was hard to walk because they were so light. They had to bounce across the ground.

Moon Weather

There is no weather on the moon. No wind blows the soil. No rain wears away the rocks. The moon looks the same today as it did millions of years ago.

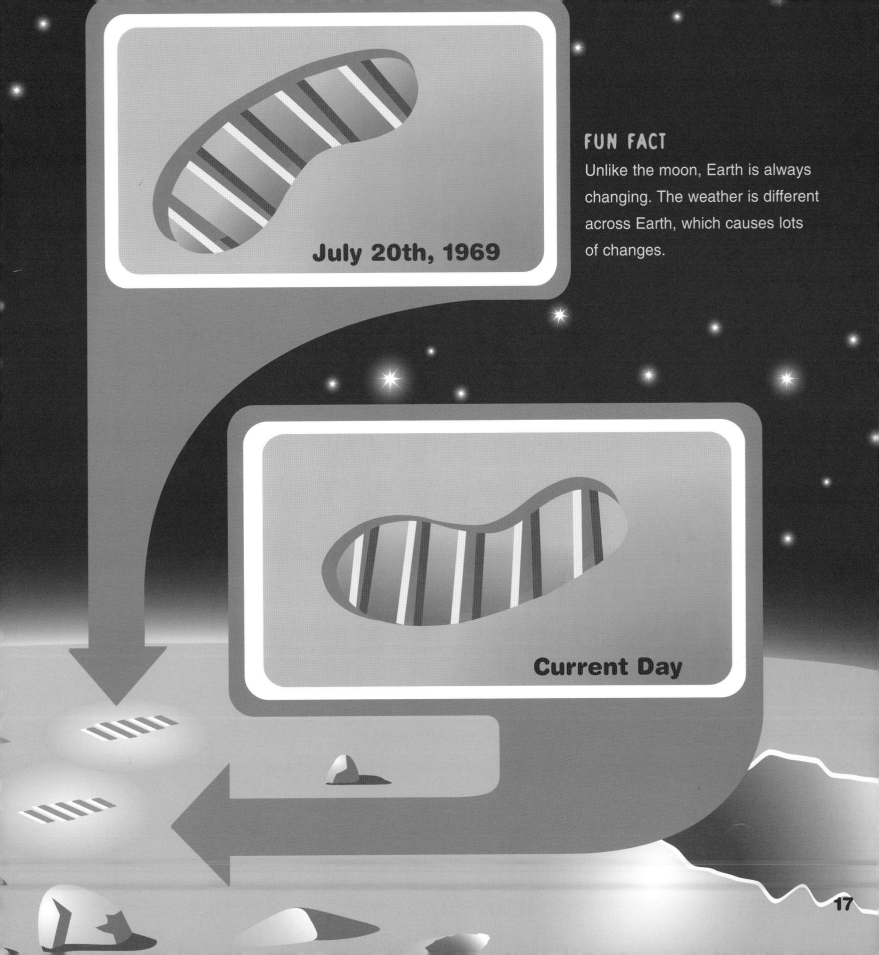

July 20th, 1969

FUN FACT
Unlike the moon, Earth is always changing. The weather is different across Earth, which causes lots of changes.

Current Day

Turning Tides

Have you ever been to the ocean? Sometimes the beach is large because the water level is low. When the water is low, it is called low tide. Sometimes the beach is small because the water level is high. When the water is high, it is called high tide.

The moon helps make tides happen. The moon pulls on Earth and pulls the water away from the beach.

FUN FACT

On most ocean shores, there is one high tide and one low tide each day. High tide might wipe out a sandcastle you made on the shore. Low tide shows the sandy ocean bottom where you might find interesting creatures to study.

Staying Together

You and your friends do things together. They stay close to you so you are not alone.

Earth and the moon are like friends. They stick close together in space.

FUN FACT

The word "month" comes from the word moon. A month is the time it takes the moon to orbit Earth once. The moon orbits Earth about twelve times a year. This is the number of months we have on our calendars.

Making Craters

What you need:

* a metal baking pan or tray with edges
* sand
* tennis ball
* golf ball
* smaller rubber ball

What you do:

1. Go outside, and fill a tray or baking pan with sand.

2. Stand above the tray and drop a tennis ball into the sand. Take it out without disturbing the sand. What type of crater did it make? Is the crater big or small? Is it bumpy or smooth?

3. Next, drop a golf ball into the sand. Then, try a small rubber ball. What types of craters did they make?

4. Stand a few feet away from the sand. Toss the balls into the sand one at a time. How are these craters different from the other ones you made?

5. Now, think about the moon. The sand is like the moon's surface. The balls are like rocks. Do you think big rocks and little rocks made different craters on the moon? Would the way a rock hit the moon change the type of crater it made?

Moon News

Growing and Shrinking

There are words for the changes of the moon. When the moon appears to be smaller, it is waning. When the moon appears to be larger, it is waxing.

On the Moon

Twelve men have visited the moon. They studied rocks and craters. Some even drove a special car over the moon's surface.

Rocky Souvenirs

Astronauts studied rocks on the moon. They also brought moon rocks back to Earth. People on Earth were able to study the rocks, too.

Big and Small

The moon is much smaller than Earth. The moon is roughly the size of Africa. Four moons lined up would be as wide as Earth.

Black Skies

Earth's sky is blue because there is air around our planet. There is no air around the moon. The moon's sky is always black, even during the day.

Glossary

astronaut—a person who travels in space

crater—a hole left behind by crashing rocks

gravity—the natural force that pulls Earth and moon toward each other

orbit—the oval-shaped path one object takes around another object in space

phases—different shapes of the moon

tides—the rising and falling of ocean water levels

To Learn More

At the Library

Branley, Franklyn M. *What the Moon Is Like.* New York: HarperCollins, 2000.

Evert, Laura. *Planets, Moons, and Stars.* Chanhassen, Minn.: Northword Press, 2003.

Wallace, Nancy Elizabeth. *The Sun, the Moon, and the Stars: Poems.* Boston: Houghton Mifflin, 2003.

On the Web

FactHound offers a safe, fun way to find Web sites related to this book. All of the sites on FactHound have been researched by our staff.

1. Visit *www.facthound.com*
2. Type in this special code: 1404811362
3. Click on the FETCH IT button.

Your trusty FactHound will fetch the best Web sites for you!

Look for all of the books in the Amazing Science: Exploring the Sky series:

Fluffy, Flat, and Wet: **A Book About Clouds**

Hot and Bright: **A Book About the Sun**

Night Light: **A Book About the Moon**

Space Leftovers: **A Book About Comets, Asteroids, and Meteoroids**

Spinning in Space: **A Book About the Planets**

Spots of Light: **A Book About Stars**